T0398509

WATER

Anna Skowrońska

Graphic design and illustrations by
Agata Dudek and Małgorzata Nowak

Translation by Antonia Lloyd-Jones

Boxer Books

50%

92%

74%

92%

45%

10%

Water is essential for manufacturing every single product, even ones you can't eat, such as an iPhone (3,400 gallons) or a T-shirt (766 gallons). It's in every portion of food. Before a hamburger reaches your plate, about 660 gallons of water will have been used to produce it. Making a cup of tea requires 8 gallons, and a bar of chocolate as many as 450 gallons. Water even forms up to 60% of the human body and over 80% of the human brain. There can be no life without it.

85%

84%

93%

70%

80%

95%

75%

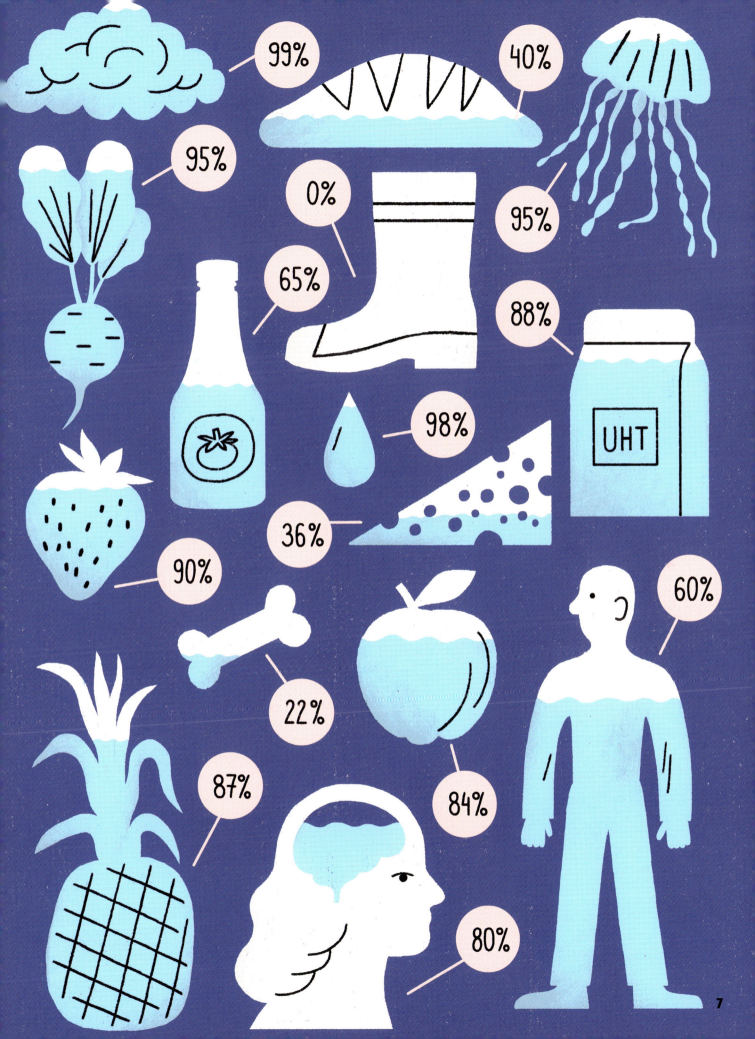

H₂O

One atom of oxygen and two atoms of hydrogen that stick together like three close friends form the molecule H_2O, the substance we know as water. Each raindrop contains many millions of molecules.

These molecules, or whole water particles, attract one another, too. The two hydrogen atoms contained in one particle of water are drawn to the oxygen atom in another. But these connections are quite weak, and as a result, they are always changing. Water particles like to hang around in groups, but they don't stay together forever. It's like a group of friends that constantly changes when new people arrive and some of the original people leave.

If you put salt in a glass of water, you'll see the salt disappear. This happens because water isn't just good at sticking to itself; it also pulls other things apart, like salt. Water can dissolve salt, oxygen, and many other substances that living things need. When water moves around, it carries these important things with it. This is how water moves nutrients through your body. Water helps life exist on Earth!

8

Water exists in three different states. The water we drink, use to make lemonade, and swim in is **liquid**. Glaciers, frozen puddles, and the ice cubes we put in the lemonade are **solids**. Invisible steam that rises in the air is known as **gas**. Water changes between these forms, and it's amazing how nature takes care of it all!

LIQUID   SOLID   GAS

HOW MUCH WATER IS THERE ON EARTH?

There's a great deal of water on Earth, more than 265 trillion gallons—and a trillion is a huge number. But not everyone can easily drink it or wash their hands with it. Some places in the world are extremely hot and dry, and others have snow all year. To make things more complicated, the overwhelming majority of all water on our planet—more than 97% of it—is **salt or ocean water**. But for drinking and washing, we need **fresh water**. It's hard to imagine that there are places where it's simply not possible to easily wash your hands because of the lack of fresh water.

NORTH AMERICA

ATLANTIC OCEAN

PACIFIC OCEAN

SOUTH AMERICA

Aysha is thirteen years old. She wakes up at 6:30 a.m., puts plastic containers on her camel, and goes to fetch water. She doesn't hurry. She walks slowly for a couple of hours. Around 11:00 she reaches the banks of a muddy river. She fills her containers and washes her face. Then she heads back home, arriving at about 4:30 p.m. Aysha lives in Ethiopia, and in some parts of Africa children often have to walk a long way to fetch water for their families. Sometimes the journey takes so long that it's impossible for the children to go to school. They usually go in groups because it's safer that way. Quite often, the only source of water in the vicinity is also used by animals and is full of silt and all sorts of bacteria. This kind of water is unhealthy to drink. Each year, more than 440,000 children under the age of five die worldwide because of acute diarrhea caused by the bacteria in dirty water.

EUROPE

ASIA

AFRICA

PACIFIC
OCEAN

INDIAN
OCEAN

AUSTRALIA

ANTARCTICA

WATER
SHORTAGE

WATER
SURFEIT

You, too, can be mindful of how much water you use each day. Did you know that every time you flush the toilet, you use approximately 1.28 gallons of water? While you're brushing your teeth, turn off the tap until you are ready to rinse. If you help to load the dishwasher, make sure it's full before you run it. Choose a quick shower rather than a bath in the tub. Before you throw away food, remember how much water was used to produce it.

A desert full of water

Most of our fresh water is to be found in Antarctica. In fact, almost the entire landscape of that continent consists of water. However, this does not mean it's easy to drink, because it's frozen solid.

A crust of ice covers the entire region, and in some parts, it is as much as 3 miles thick. Additionally, in winter ice forms on the surface of the surrounding waters as well, extending for many miles. A desert of ice stretches far inland, where the temperature can be as low as minus 76°F. It never rains there, and the snow that occasionally falls turns into ice. As a result, although the whole area is full of frozen water, it is extremely dry. There are no cities or villages, and no countries on this icy continent.

The only inhabited sites in Antarctica are the international polar stations, where scientists work. They are interested in studying the habits of the region's wildlife, and they also monitor the ice to see if it is increasing or decreasing, because the amount of ice affects the whole planet's climate. Ice reflects solar rays more powerfully than the largest ocean surfaces. When ice melts, fewer rays bounce back into the cosmos, and the climate grows warmer. This is why scientists have been monitoring the state of the sea ice in the Arctic and around Antarctica for many years.

Try to say the following words aloud quickly: *Antarctica, the Antarctic, the Arctic.* It sounds like a tongue twister, but these are the names of some of the coldest places on Earth. The Arctic is the northernmost part of our planet. It includes the frozen Arctic Ocean and islands such as Greenland, as well as the northern coasts of Europe, Asia, and North America. Different parts of the Arctic belong to different countries. The people who have lived there for a long time used to be known as Eskimos, but now they prefer to be called the Inuit. Various animals live there, the largest of which is the polar bear. While the name "Antarctica" refers to the continent, "the Antarctic" describes the area that includes Antarctica, the Southern Ocean, and a large number of islands. In this region, penguins are the best-known animal.

On King George Island off the coast of Antarctica, the Henryk Arctowski Polish Antarctic Station conducts scientific research. In summer, as many as forty people work there. At the end of March, with the onset of winter, it is almost always dark, which makes it nearly impossible to work outside, so only ten employees at most remain at the station. They are more than 8,700 miles away from home. Sometimes severe weather forces them to stay indoors for weeks at a time, with no chance of breathing fresh air. The biting wind blows at a speed of up to 155 miles per hour, making the walls of their homes, and everything inside, shake. To keep themselves comfortable and entertained, the station's residents come up with fun things to do. For instance, they celebrate some special holidays, play board games, and cook interesting meals. The polar scientists also learned to apply these experiences of life to the lockdowns during the COVID-19 pandemic. They were able to share tips with others on how to keep busy and stay positive when stuck inside.

In 2024, the Polish Antarctic Station gained a new building designed by a firm of architects named Kuryłowicz & Associates. It's hard to build in a place where extreme winter conditions prevail for most of the year, so the new house for the polar scientists sailed to its destination on a ship in ready-made pieces that can easily be assembled and installed, like a toy house made of building blocks.
The new base has a sauna, a swimming pool, and even a greenhouse where the scientists will be able to grow vegetables.

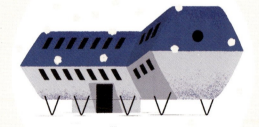

Do you remember when the White Witch made it always winter in Narnia, but Christmas never happened? In his book *The Lion, the Witch and the Wardrobe*, C. S. Lewis described deep, permanent snow and ice-bound streams. He was very good at describing winter in words, while the Polish artist Julian Fałat was very good at painting it. He was brilliant at capturing the various shades of snow.

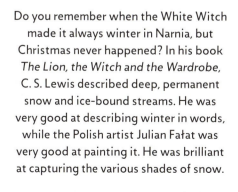

AN OCEAN IN THE AIR

Can water from the Vistula River in Poland make its way to Russia? Can water from the Mediterranean Sea reach Norway? Can water from the Atlantic Ocean travel to India? Yes. Thanks to solar energy, water evaporates every day from rivers and oceans. As a result, water from a river that flows near your home can end up in an entirely different part of the world.

Compared with the quantity of water that exists on land, there is not much of it in the air. But water in the form of vapor does have an advantage: it can move a long way rapidly. In the right weather conditions, rain, snow, or hail falls from the clouds, causing the water to soak back into the soil or fall back into rivers, streams, and oceans. Later on, it evaporates again and is carried from rivers, seas, and oceans back into the air. Water's constant journey through evaporation, condensation, clouds, and rainfall is one of the elements that forms the climate.

And do you know how trees contribute to this process? They source water from underground through their roots, and then, with the help of their leaves, they release it into the atmosphere in the form of steam. If there are lots of trees, they become real "producers" of moisture and can help to generate rain.

Evaporation

Have you ever seen raindrops on the pavement vanishing, or puddles drying up? When exposed to heat, water particles move faster and faster until finally they break the connections that bind them and take off, like planes from a runway. Liquid changes into gas. As it evaporates, the water takes the thermal energy with it and carries it until it changes into drops of liquid or ice crystals within a cloud. Then it is released. There's even a special name for this phenomenon: **latent heat**.

Perspiration

Your body uses water to cool down. In hot weather, it doesn't want to overheat, so it sweats. As the water that forms sweat evaporates, it removes heat from the body and releases it into the atmosphere.

THE SUN IN THE OCEAN

Even if you live hundreds of miles from the ocean, it has a constant effect on your life. As you read this book, the ocean never stops supplying the atmosphere with moisture and globally distributing the energy that comes from the Sun. It creates our climate, and it has the power to do so because of its immense size. Almost all the water we have on Earth is collected in the oceans—about 96.5% of it. Every day, a vast quantity of oxygen is formed there. It's largely produced by microscopic plants that would be hard to see if they didn't live in colonies. Moved around by the flow of the water, they rise to the ocean's surface. This is called phytoplankton, which nourishes itself by drawing carbon dioxide from the air and releasing oxygen. Phytoplankton is a tasty treat for krill—tiny creatures that resemble transparent shrimp and weigh at most 0.07 ounces. Krill in turn are food for whales. The biggest whale, the blue whale, is capable of swimming thousands of miles in search of krill in the cold depths off the coast of Antarctica. Every day, it can eat several tons of these creatures.

And so, microscopic phytoplankton makes a meal for krill, and krill end up in the jaws of massive whales. When whales eat, some leftovers fall to the ocean floor and they look like snowflakes. As a result, they are known as marine snow. When it lands on the ocean bed, it becomes food for deep-sea organisms. In the ocean, everything is connected, so nothing goes to waste.

PHYTOPLANKTON

KRILL

Blue Planet
If you look at a map of the world, you'll see that water takes up far more space than land—about 71% of the Earth's surface. That's why in photographs from outer space our planet looks blue. As for volume, 96.5% of all the water on our planet is found in seas and oceans, 1.7% in glaciers and permanent snow, and another 1.7% in underground waters. The rest, about 0.1%, is in rivers, lakes, streams, puddles, living organisms, and the air in the form of clouds or water vapor.

MOTION IN THE OCEAN

A team of scientists conducted research in the waters of the Pacific Ocean off the coast of Panama. Divers equipped a camera to follow a jellyfish. They used a laser to illuminate the ocean depths, while at the same time releasing a dye that helped them to trace the water motion caused by the animal. They measured the movement of the tiny particles rising around it. They calculated how many gallons of water a jellyfish can stir with one forward motion and how this quantity changes depending on the size of the creature and the way it moves. What happens if ten, one hundred, or one thousand jellyfish, sardines, or tuna fish appear at once?

The ocean is like a gigantic solar panel. Every day, it absorbs solar energy, which it stores and then releases into the atmosphere or transfers along with the water. Animals have a role to play in this process. A whale, a tuna fish, even a small sardine or a jellyfish can stir the ocean water as it swims along, setting them in motion.

Animals contribute to water motion, but most of the work is done by sea currents. Vast quantities of water are constantly shifting in the ocean. One of the reasons for this is a difference in temperature. If you pour cold water into one bottle and hot water into another, you won't see any difference between them with the naked eye. Meanwhile, the particles in the bottle of cold water are more crowded and more numerous. This water is heavier. So, if it's poured into hotter water, it will sink to the bottom and push the hotter water to the top. The same thing happens with fresh and salt water. Salt water is denser, so it sinks, too, pushing the fresh water upward.

That's why the water in the oceans and seas never stops moving around. Wherever warm water regularly meets cold water, or saltier water meets less-salty water, marine currents are formed. They're a bit like powerful rivers inside oceans that are constantly flowing along well-worn paths. For thousands of years they've been distributing solar energy, oxygen, and nutrients around the world, which allows the creatures and plants living in the ocean to grow and develop. Warm waters in the region of the Equator flow toward the North and South Poles, where they mix with cold waters. Cooled down, they sink to the depths and return toward the Equator, where they come back up to the surface. They flow majestically, mixing the upper levels with those that the sun never reaches. Thanks to solar rays and plants, oxygen is produced in the upper levels of the ocean. The waters sinking to the lower levels carry it down to places where the light cannot reach. This allows living organisms to grow in the depths. These currents are sometimes referred to as **the global conveyor belt.**

Salinity
There is one sea where you can lie down in the water and it will hold you up. This is the Dead Sea in Israel. The water is very salty and, as a result, so dense that a person won't sink in it. You don't have to swim to stay on the surface. Instead, you can just lie there reading a book or simply doing nothing.

EAST
ANTARCTICA

GLACIER

THE
SOUTH POLE

WEST
ANTARCTICA

MOUNT EREBUS,
ACTIVE VOLCANO
(12,448 FT ABOVE SEA LEVEL)

The Antarctic Circumpolar Current

Strong, steady winds blow across the water and make
it move. A cold current caused by western winds flows
idly around the Antarctic, and it takes around three
years to complete one loop. Although it's not fast,
it reaches the depths and moves enormous quantities
of water. It mixes warm and cold waters and is known as
the Antarctic Circumpolar Current.

The Pacific Ocean
If we were to join all the lands on Earth together, their surface would still be smaller than the Pacific Ocean. This ocean stretches from the Arctic to Antarctica, with its waves reaching the coasts of Australia, North and South America, and Asia in between. At its deepest point, it goes down almost 6.8 miles. Ferdinand Magellan, who in 1520 sailed across the ocean in fine weather, named it the "pacific" — the peaceful sea. The name stuck, and that's what we still call it, but it would be hard to imagine less-peaceful waters. This is where the most violent tropical cyclones, known as hurricanes, arise. They bring waves as tall as houses, and winds that can outrace the fastest cars.

High and low tides

If we run along the sand at the edge of the ocean in the morning, we might find that the same track a few hours later will be underwater because the high tide will have flooded the beach. And a few more hours later, the water will withdraw again. These regular movements of the ocean are caused by the moon's gravitational pull. In some places, the sea moves more than a dozen yards, while in others, it moves just a few inches. When the water and tourists leave the beach, along come the treasure hunters with metal detectors. But they're more likely to find tin cans and bottle caps than gold.

THE MARIANA TRENCH

Although the ocean has such a major effect on our lives, our knowledge of it is limited. Journeys to great depths are difficult and dangerous, because the deeper down you go, the greater the pressure exerted by the water. And there are places where it is unimaginably deep. If Mount Everest were submerged in the Mariana Trench, its summit would disappear underwater.

While hundreds of expeditions have reached the top of the world's highest mountain, only twenty-two have reached the world's deepest point. In 2012, James Cameron set off on an unusual journey, aiming to travel almost 6.8 miles underwater, to the very bottom of the Pacific Ocean, where there is no light. At dawn, one day in March, he boarded his bathyscaphe, a small submersible, or boat, used for deep-sea exploration, and headed straight into the darkness. He sat curled up with his knees under his chin in the small watertight cabin, because that was all the space available for the pilot. The underwater darkness was lit up by powerful external headlights, making it possible to use film cameras. Cameron was able to monitor changes in the water temperature and the speed at which his green, rocket-like submersible was descending. After traveling vertically downward for two hours and thirty-six minutes he landed safely at the bottom, with 6.8 miles of water towering above him. Underneath him was the ocean bed, just slightly disturbed by contact with the bathyscaphe. The powerful lamps lit up the underwater wasteland. There were no signs of life. Cameron activated external robots that were to collect samples from the ocean bed and went on a horizontal journey, filming and observing the almost-lunar landscape. After almost three hours, he began his preparations for returning to the surface. To rise up again, he had to discard two 536 pound weights. Half a ton lighter, the submersible sprang from the ocean bed at lightning speed and seventy minutes later, it surfaced into blazing sunlight. The last time someone had reached the bottom of the Mariana Trench was fifty-two years earlier, though on that occasion, in a less advanced version of a bathyscaphe, the mission was shorter—only twenty minutes—with no opportunity to collect samples.

MARIANA TRENCH

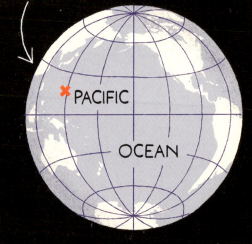

PACIFIC

OCEAN

FIN

LIGHTING

BATTERIES

CAMERA

PILOT'S CABIN

BALLAST

LIGHTING

James Cameron is a Canadian movie director. His most famous movie is about the sinking of the *Titanic*. This love story set on board the tragic ship brought Cameron fame and Oscar awards. But he is not just a creative artist; he is also fascinated by exploration. He spent seven years preparing for his journey to the bottom of the Mariana Trench. He co-designed and supervised the construction of his submersible. Now he is cooperating with NASA, the US space agency, on the "conquest" of Mars.

MICROPLASTIC

THE GREAT PACIFIC GARBAGE PATCH

It's difficult to imagine a garbage heap larger than the size of New Mexico. And yet there is an area within the Pacific where garbage drifts on the surface of the water and is tossed by the waves until it sinks, only to float up again and reappear in a completely different spot. "Ghost nets" thrown away by fishermen become traps for fish and other creatures. This area is known as the Great Pacific Garbage Patch, and it lies in between California and Hawaii. It is the biggest, but not the only, drifting garbage heap in the ocean.

If someone throws a plastic bottle into the sea, the waves will churn it up for years, grinding it into microscopic pieces that get into the bellies of mackerel, salmon, and all sorts of other marine creatures.
These fish and crustaceans are then caught and sold in shops, from where they reach our kitchens. And so, along with a delicious dinner, we end up eating some invisible specks of plastic.

MICROPLASTIC

Garbage ground by great masses of water breaks down into ever tinier pieces, only a few of which can be seen with the naked eye. 95% of them are no bigger than a grain of pepper. It's hard to gather something that's impossible to see and that never stops changing place. Your great-great-grandchildren will still be coming across single-use plastic plates and cups that we throw away today, because they won't truly disappear for several hundred years. People do not realize that as they sunbathe on sandy beaches, they are partly lying on tiny specks of plastic mixed in with the grains of sand. Swimming in a sea of plastic, fish, crabs, seahorses, dolphins, and other marine creatures are dying because of this pollution. The extent of littering is now so great that various campaigns are being organized to clean it up.

The ambitious project of a Dutch teenager

Boyan Slat was 16 and diving off the coast of Greece when he noticed that there was more plastic than there were fish in the water. "Why don't we just clean it up?" he wondered. His questions led to a high school science project, which led to him presenting his ideas at a conference. Months later, Boyan left college and founded The Ocean Cleanup. The video of his presentation went viral—hundreds of thousands of people watched it. He was able to assemble a team that included scientists and engineers to devise a method for cleaning the oceans. They invented some very long floating barriers, arranged in the shape of the letters *U* or *V* which were towed along the surface of the ocean, gathering up plastic and other rubbish. In 2019, the innovative cleaning system caught its first batch of plastic. Some plastic is studied and some is responsibly recycled. And Ocean Cleanup is not just cleaning up oceans, but the world's rivers as well.

Plastic at a depth of almost 6.8 miles? It sounds weird, and yet . . . in 2019, American businessman Victor Vescovo descended in a bathyscaphe to the bottom of the Mariana Trench. At the deepest point in the world, he found a plastic bag and candy wrappers!

UNDERWATER TREASURES

Imagine a scene in which fish are swimming around ancient statues, brushing against stone tablets that are hardly visible beneath a coating of crustaceans. There are toppled columns lying on the seabed, in pitch darkness, lit only by divers' flashlights. Is this the legendary Atlantis? No, it's a real ancient Egyptian city, and its name is Thonis-Heracleion. For 1,200 years, it has been hidden approximately 33 feet below the surface of Abu Qir Bay.

At one time, the Nile River flowed into the Mediterranean Sea at this point. The river's life-giving waters flooded the neighboring fields, irrigating them. Thonis-Heracleion buzzed with life. Ships carrying goods called at the port. Statues of the Egyptian gods stood motionless, staring into space. But then, for reasons that can't be fully explained, the sea engulfed the city. For twelve centuries, all trace of it was lost. The statues, tablets, and temples were covered by sand and overgrown with algae.

In 1933, a British pilot flying overhead spotted part of the underwater ruins. But it wasn't until the year 2000 that the French marine archaeologist Franck Goddio discovered the long-forgotten city. He and his team of divers excavated the site, clearing away the sand and uncovering pieces of the sculptures. The smaller objects were brought to the surface in special bags, while the statues and tablets were hauled onto the deck of a ship using a crane. Now they are in a museum in Cairo.

Marine archaeologists are experts in art and history, but they also have to be extremely good at diving, as that is the only way to reach treasures hidden underwater. When divers descend, they must overcome the resistance of the water, which is eight hundred times denser than air. As the sea rises higher and higher above them, its weight presses down on them. Their bodies have to adapt to this. But the return journey is even worse, and surfacing is the most dangerous moment of all. The divers have to be careful to return to the surface very slowly, to allow their bodies to adapt to the reduction in pressure gradually.

PRESSURE

To imagine water pressure, find an empty plastic bottle and make three holes in it: one right at the bottom, one in the middle, and one near the top. Pour water into the bottle and look what happens: from which hole is the stream of water strongest? You'll find that it's the one at the bottom, because that's where the greatest amount of water is exerting pressure. So, the more water there is above you, the more pressure is pushing down on you.

In the past, divers could only stay underwater for as long as they could hold their breath. Now they breathe using oxygen cylinders. But there are still fans of diving without oxygen who attempt to break the record for the longest and deepest dive.

Sometimes divers study underwater life beneath the ice. As we know, particles of frozen water are less compressed than they are in a liquid state. As a result, ice rises to the surface, and animals and plants can live beneath the frozen surface of seas, lakes, and rivers. To observe them, divers jump into holes cut into the ice. Then they have to be careful not to lose their way back to them—that's the only exit to the surface!

Divers, movie makers, and tourists go on underwater expeditions with dolphins, beluga whales, and even sharks. To keep safe from man-eating sharks, they get into a metal cage that's lowered into the water from a boat.

And did you know that for more than 1,200 years, mothers in Japan have passed on to their daughters the tradition of diving in search of pearls and seafood? Nowadays, their numbers are dwindling, but there are women in their eighties who still dive in white linen costumes. They are known as ama.

WEALTH SAILING ON WATER

We travel by car, train, or plane, but in the past, people sailed on ships or boats, and floated cargo on rafts. For our ancestors, rivers, lakes, and seas were "highways." The journeys took weeks, or sometimes months. Countries that had a good fleet were strong and rich.

Ancient Mesopotamia did not have many natural resources, such as deposits of gold or other metals. Its wealth was two great rivers—the Tigris and the Euphrates. An ideal network of canals was also built inland, thanks to which the fields were irrigated but not flooded. The waterways also served to transport various goods, which allowed trade to develop. The country imported goods and quickly became rich.

In 1492, Christopher Columbus sailed from a port in the Canary Islands. He headed westward, aiming to reach India. He was trying to find a fast sea route to Asia, from where European merchants imported fabrics, spices, and tea. The Portuguese had already charted eastern routes by sailing around Africa, but the journey took around six months. Columbus had major ambitions. He persuaded the Spanish king and queen to finance his bold idea of traveling to India in just a few weeks. He set out with three ships, and after three months, he and his crew reached unfamiliar land. Columbus thought it was India. At the time, he had no idea that he had found an entirely unknown continent. According to the law in those days, all newly discovered lands not inhabited by Christians were claimed by the state that had discovered them.

Columbus declared it to be the property of the Kingdom of Spain. Soon after, the Spanish set out for the conquest of America.

Over the next century, Spain became even more powerful. Elizabeth I, queen of England, knew that she could only conquer Spain by gaining the advantage on the seas. So, she supported Francis Drake's pirate expeditions, and allowed him to plunder Spanish ships off the coast of Latin America. When the Spanish tried to invade England, the English ships carried off a splendid victory over the Spanish Armada. From then on, the English fleet grew in strength and acquired colonies all over the world.

CANALS

Journeys to the east by ship continued for a long time. They were expensive and dangerous. Wanting faster access to their colonies in Asia, the British thought up some shortcuts. In the nineteenth century, they joined the Mediterranean Sea and the Red Sea by building a canal. It took thousands of people ten years to build the Suez Canal, thanks to which the journey was reduced by half. In many parts of the world, canals are dug to create faster and easier ways to travel. Sometimes this worries ecologists, who are concerned that these activities can do harm to nature.

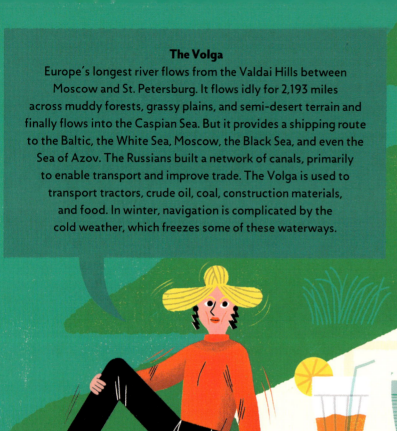

The Volga
Europe's longest river flows from the Valdai Hills between Moscow and St. Petersburg. It flows idly for 2,193 miles across muddy forests, grassy plains, and semi-desert terrain and finally flows into the Caspian Sea. But it provides a shipping route to the Baltic, the White Sea, Moscow, the Black Sea, and even the Sea of Azov. The Russians built a network of canals, primarily to enable transport and improve trade. The Volga is used to transport tractors, crude oil, coal, construction materials, and food. In winter, navigation is complicated by the cold weather, which freezes some of these waterways.

Nowadays, rice, wheat, soy, coffee, and many other goods sail to our kitchens from distant continents. Air transport would be too expensive, so many products sail on specially designed ships known as containers. The biggest ones are as long as almost four football pitches (1,380 feet). They can carry more than twenty-three thousand containers, which a system of cranes places in even rows like toy bricks. One empty container weighs more than three tons. Fruit and vegetables sail in freezer trucks and liquids in tankers. For cars, there are special containers equipped with "shelves" for the vehicles to sit on, safely attached so they won't shift around from the rocking of the waves. Ships of every size carry cargo intercontinentally, following a small number of routes, known as shipping lanes.

COFFEE FROM COLOMBIA

APPLES FROM POLAND

GRAPES FROM SOUTH AFRICA

BANANAS FROM ECUADOR

PEANUTS FROM CHINA

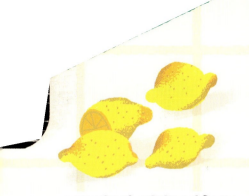

LEMONS FROM SPAIN

WATERMELONS
FROM ITALY

SALMON FROM
NORWAY

PINEAPPLES
FROM
COSTA RICA

CHOCOLATES
FROM GERMANY

WINE FROM
FRANCE

GARLIC FROM
CHINA

STRAWBERRIES
FROM THE USA

BUTTON MUSHROOMS
FROM POLAND

AVOCADOS
FROM MEXICO

WHEAT FROM INDIA

Water is not just needed to transport goods. Before they reach our homes, apples, pants, shoes, bread, rice, and many other products use water. It's called "virtual" water, because it doesn't exist physically within the given product, but it was used to make it. Before a pound of rice reaches the cooking pot, it uses about 330 gallons of water. In Asia rice is cultivated by people, not machines. First, they sow the seeds in special beds. Once the seeds have sprouted, they transplant the seedlings to fields, wading in water up to their ankles. Rice needs a lot of water. It is planted during the summer monsoon season, when warm, moist air is blowing from the ocean toward the land, bringing heavy rains. When the harvest comes, the farmers cut the stems and then thresh the grains to separate them from the chaff. Once it's ready to sell, the rice sails away on ships.

RICE

Nearly 4,000 gallons of water is needed to produce about 2 pounds of beef. Why so much? Because the figure includes not just the water the cow drinks but also the water needed to cultivate and produce its fodder and to clean the cowshed, as well as the water that will be polluted during many years of cattle farming.

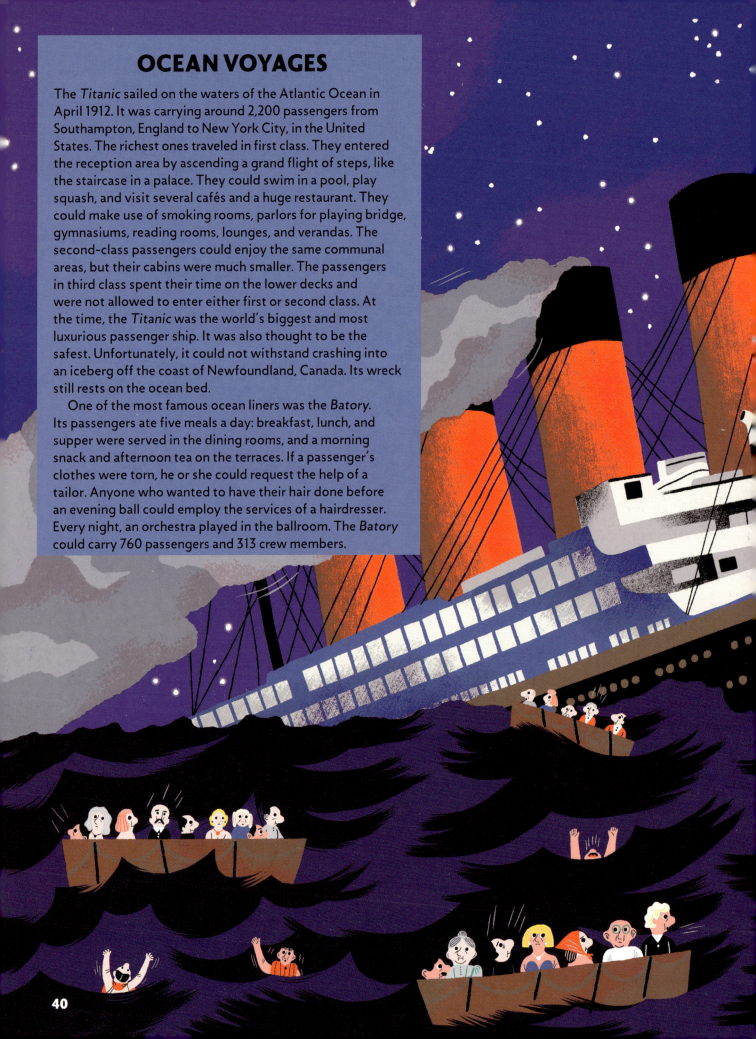

OCEAN VOYAGES

The *Titanic* sailed on the waters of the Atlantic Ocean in April 1912. It was carrying around 2,200 passengers from Southampton, England to New York City, in the United States. The richest ones traveled in first class. They entered the reception area by ascending a grand flight of steps, like the staircase in a palace. They could swim in a pool, play squash, and visit several cafés and a huge restaurant. They could make use of smoking rooms, parlors for playing bridge, gymnasiums, reading rooms, lounges, and verandas. The second-class passengers could enjoy the same communal areas, but their cabins were much smaller. The passengers in third class spent their time on the lower decks and were not allowed to enter either first or second class. At the time, the *Titanic* was the world's biggest and most luxurious passenger ship. It was also thought to be the safest. Unfortunately, it could not withstand crashing into an iceberg off the coast of Newfoundland, Canada. Its wreck still rests on the ocean bed.

One of the most famous ocean liners was the *Batory*. Its passengers ate five meals a day: breakfast, lunch, and supper were served in the dining rooms, and a morning snack and afternoon tea on the terraces. If a passenger's clothes were torn, he or she could request the help of a tailor. Anyone who wanted to have their hair done before an evening ball could employ the services of a hairdresser. Every night, an orchestra played in the ballroom. The *Batory* could carry 760 passengers and 313 crew members.

Kayaker Aleksander Doba sailed across the Atlantic without any orchestras, ballrooms, hairdressers, or tailors. He crossed the ocean three times, solo, in a kayak. He had no motor, just his own two hands, a paddle, and roughly 13 square feet of space. In May 2017, he set off on his final voyage from New York, and in September he reached the coast of France. In 110 days, he had sailed approximately 4,970 miles, a journey that can be made comfortably by plane in a few hours. His route ran across the northern part of the Atlantic, which is famous for cold, foggy days and extremely strong winds. During one storm, the kayak was tossed by waves several feet high, and the wind raced at a speed of more than 60 miles per hour. Along the way, sharks quite often followed the kayak, circling around the helm. Aleksander Doba actually stroked one of them. He completed his final voyage shortly before his seventy-first birthday.

THIRD TRANSATLANTIC VOYAGE

SECOND TRANSATLANTIC VOYAGE

OLO

FIRST TRANSATLANTIC VOYAGE

The Atlantic Ocean
The waters of the Atlantic stretch from the Arctic to the Antarctic. They join both Americas with Europe and Africa. Hundreds of years ago, favorable winds brought navigators that way, allowing them to discover new lands. More recently, the Aquarius Reef Base, an undersea marine laboratory located on the Atlantic sea floor off the coast of Florida, is helping to prepare for major discoveries in outer space. There, engineers, scientists, and astronauts are taught to acclimatise to conditions similar to those they will encounter in the cosmos.

INHABITANTS OF THE OCEAN

Australian box jelly

In the Baltic Sea, you can find jellyfish with a transparent, round "umbrella." But there are also jellyfish that have a square umbrella, like a box. Of these, the Australian box jellyfish is the deadliest, and can be found along Australia's northern coastline. It is also known as the sea wasp, or the marine stinger.

Anglerfish

Anglerfish can live deep down near the sea bottom, where the light never reaches. Their large mouths and sharp teeth make it easier to catch prey, which can be scarce. Females have a special lure on their head. The end of the fishing rod-like lure has bacteria inside that emit light that in turn attract prey.

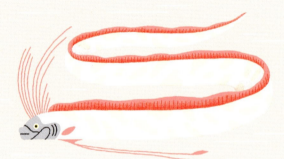

Giant oarfish

This is a fish that looks like an enormous snake and can grow to become over 26 feet long. Its head is topped with a red crest, and it has a red dorsal fin stretching the length of its body. By rippling this fin, the oarfish can rise vertically in the water.

Bluefin tuna

We're used to seeing tuna in a can, so not everyone realizes how big these fish are. They can weigh up to 770 pounds and be up to 8 feet long. Bluefin tuna is considered so delicious that some people will spend a fortune on it. In 2019, the owner of a chain of Japanese sushi restaurants paid more than three million dollars for a 612-pound specimen. Tuna fishing has become so competitive that some species of this fish are now on the red list of endangered species.

Great white shark

This is a very clever creature. It can smell blood from several hundred feet away. When it hunts, it furtively swims up to its victim from below and attacks suddenly, with such force and speed that it jumps clear of the water. It has three hundred teeth with which it bites chunks of flesh off its victim, swallowing the pieces whole.

Flying fish

While some fish jump out of the water to catch their prey, others do it to save themselves from predators. Flying fish have large front fins, which allow them to glide through the air. Able to fly over a distance of up to 656 feet, they can avoid being attacked from underwater.

Blue whale

This is the world's largest animal. Its heart alone can weigh up to around 1,500 pounds. Many blue whales spend the summer in polar waters, because that's where they can find the most food in that season. The whale opens its mouth wide, letting in water containing krill. Then it closes its jaws until the baleen—long plates of horny bristles that hang from its palate—covers the opening and lets out the water through the gaps between the bristles, as if through a sieve. Only the filtered food remains in its mouth.

Coral

Seahorses, clown fish, turtles, mussels, crayfish, and many other marine species make their home on reefs, which are created by other creatures: corals. An individual coral is the shape of a small pipe, with a mouth opening at the top end surrounded by many feelers. A colony of corals looks like a brightly colored bush. Their chalky skeletons form the reef.

Octopus

These are very strange creatures. The blue blood that flows in their veins pumps three hearts. They have the largest brains of all invertebrates, but there are even more neurons (cells that make up the brain) located in their eight tentacles. If attacked, an octopus can cast off one of its tentacles, which will go on moving on its own, distracting the predator while the octopus tries to hide. For this purpose, it is able to change not just its skin color at rapid speed, but also its structure —one moment it's smooth, and the next it looks like spiky coral. And in time, the tentacle grows back.

Bivalve

Some bivalves contain hidden treasure. The shell of a pearl oyster is filled with a thick layer of mother-of-pearl. If a small grain of sand gets inside it, over time, mother-of-pearl accumulates around it, creating a pearl. The world's biggest bivalve is the giant clam. It can weigh more than 600 pounds and its shell can reach almost 5 feet long. Unfortunately, it doesn't produce pearls.

RIVERS

Some rivers flow from underground sources, while others flow from melting glaciers or lakes. Some flow fast, others slowly. In some, the water flows all year round, and in others, it dries up for a while, then reappears after torrential rains. In keeping with gravity, all rivers flow downhill. They end their course in the seas or oceans. There are thousands of them worldwide. Although it is not salt water, the water in rivers carries many mineral salts rinsed out of rocks and the ground. Sometimes this causes its color

to change. One of the longest rivers in China has its sources in Tibet at an altitude above 13,123 feet. It races down to the Loess Plateau, rinsing out rocks with ease. From this point, it carries yellow dust that gives it an intense color. That is why it is called Huang He—the Yellow River. Tons of silt then pours onto the plains and fertilizes the soil. But the river is capricious and often floods, destroying agricultural fields.

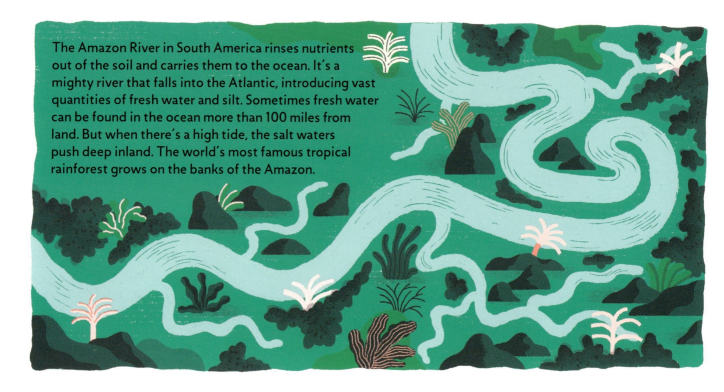

The Amazon River in South America rinses nutrients out of the soil and carries them to the ocean. It's a mighty river that falls into the Atlantic, introducing vast quantities of fresh water and silt. Sometimes fresh water can be found in the ocean more than 100 miles from land. But when there's a high tide, the salt waters push deep inland. The world's most famous tropical rainforest grows on the banks of the Amazon.

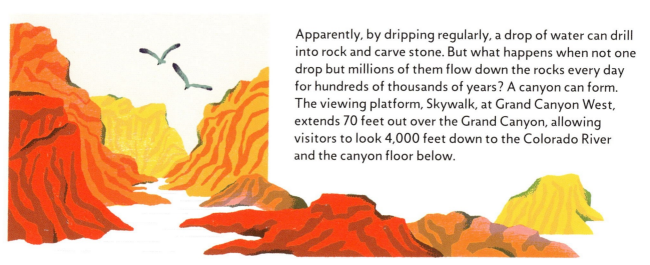

Apparently, by dripping regularly, a drop of water can drill into rock and carve stone. But what happens when not one drop but millions of them flow down the rocks every day for hundreds of thousands of years? A canyon can form. The viewing platform, Skywalk, at Grand Canyon West, extends 70 feet out over the Grand Canyon, allowing visitors to look 4,000 feet down to the Colorado River and the canyon floor below.

ASHES

Millions of people gather each year by the Ganges River. Followers of the Hindu religion come to wash away their sins in the waters of their most sacred river. On the riverbanks, there are cremation sites, and the ashes of the dead are thrown straight into the water.

The stretch of the Niagara River that connects Lakes Erie and Ontario also marks a section of the border between Canada and the USA. Roughly halfway between the two lakes, the river falls hundreds of feet. Niagara Falls is the greatest waterfall in North America, attracting millions of tourists each year. In the past, thrill-seekers used to go there, too. They would try to walk across the frozen waterfall, or jump it in a barrel. But too many accidents occurred, and now such daredevil feats are forbidden.

Dissolution

Water dissolves not just salt or sugar, but also some rocks. As it keeps washing away at a stone, it rinses out part of its substance. The stone wastes away, becoming smaller, while the water carries off various mineral salts. In a similar way, water washes fertilizers and pesticides out of the fields. Thanks to the effect of rain, the invisible pollutants that settle on plants, roads, and soil are also dissolved. The flowing water carries them off to canals and rivers. The rivers on which villages, towns, and cultivated fields lie are the most vulnerable to contamination. The water you release from the tap flows into your home along pipes, and for many of you, it is specially cleaned—for many others, the water must be boiled before it is safe to drink. Water is a good solvent, but not all substances dissolve in it. The crude oil that leaks out of shipwrecked tankers flows to the surface. The waves carry it over great distances. It sticks to birds, sea turtles, and other creatures that accidentally encounter it. It clogs their fur and feathers. Water cannot wash it off. The animals try in vain to clean themselves, and in the process, they lick off the oil, which makes them fall sick and die. Crude oil is very hard to remove, and its harmful effects last for decades.

GREAT WATER CATASTROPHES

Once in a while, deep below the waters of the Pacific Ocean, there is an earthquake. The earthquake causes waves. At first they're small and imperceptible, but they spread at the speed of a jet. They can move as fast as 620 miles per hour, covering several hundred miles. When they reach the shore, they put on the brakes because they run into an obstacle—this is where the ocean bed rises. At this point, they bank up, reaching a height of up to 100 to 150 feet, as high as a two-story house. They don't resemble ordinary waves that rise and break, one after another, but advance in a single, mighty block of water that literally submerges and destroys everything in its path and rams its way far inland. This is called a tsunami. After a while, the water recedes, churning up everything it has already seized, and then comes back again with great force.

Spiders are highly skilled at evacuating during a flood. They latch onto the smallest piece of twig or grass that's protruding from the water and spin a web on it. Then they bounce off it like a trampoline and blow away on a silken thread carried by the wind.

In the first book in the *Lord of the Rings* trilogy, *The Fellowship of the Ring,* the waters of the Bruinen River gather violently, not because of a cloudburst, but thanks to the spells of Elrond, ruler of the elves (and in the movie, it's the spells of Arwen, his daughter, too). The river sweeps away the Black Riders and their horses. The author of the books was the English writer J. R. R. Tolkien, and the movies based on them were directed by New Zealander Peter Jackson. In the screen version, the waters of the Bruinen were represented by the Arrow River in New Zealand.

FLOODS

High in the air, water vapor moves along with the wind. An aerial "river" of this kind can be extremely long, wide, and full of moisture. When it forms into clouds, it can cause torrential rain. Then, instead of soaking into the earth or flowing away, the water simply doesn't fit in the beds of streams and rivers, and the earth is not capable of absorbing such a large amount of it. The water accumulates and spills over the surrounding area, resulting in a flood.

Sometimes just fields are submerged, and the nearest houses are only partly flooded, but sometimes entire villages or towns are inundated. A tropical storm can cause flooding, too. During one of these storms, a strong wind blows from the sea or ocean, pushing vast quantities of water inland. Waves that are several feet high force their way into towns and villages with great force, destroying houses, cars, and shops.

Drought

Cape Town is situated on a bay where the waters of the Indian Ocean and the Atlantic Ocean meet. Every day, waves break against the shore, but their roaring is not reassuring. The city suffers from a lack of water. In 2018, the residents calculated when day zero would come and the water would stop flowing from their taps. The government gradually introduced various restrictions. People were only allowed to use at most 13 gallons of water daily. That's roughly enough to take a shower for ninety seconds, cook one meal, flush the toilet twice, and use a little water to wash your hands and face. The ocean sparkled in the sunlight, but the salt water was of no help, because desalination— the process for removing salt—is too expensive. People stood in lines at deep wells and at supermarkets, but sales there were limited, too. Later on, they were only allowed to take a shower twice a week.

Have you ever heard of water-saving toilet cisterns? For years manufacturers have been designing new solutions, so that toilet flushes, showers, and watering systems will use less water but still do their job. In some parts of the world, some products carry labels that say "water friendly," which means the appliance in question doesn't waste it.

There are more and more places in the world where each year more water is being used than nature can replenish. This is the case in California, Australia, and many parts of Africa. When there's no rain for weeks on end, ground water is not replenished, the soil dries out, and rivers, streams, ponds, and lakes become very shallow. Over time, underground springs also run dry. Often the earth cracks for lack of moisture. A drought can be so major that animals have nothing to drink and plants wither and die.

In this climate, fires can easily break out, but there's no water to extinguish them.

Human beings can keep going without food for approximately one month, but without water they can only survive for a week at most. Farming animals and growing vegetables, fruit, and crops requires vast amounts of water. When a drought occurs, unlike a storm or a cloudburst, it has a gradual effect, but the damage it causes is very hard to repair.

UNDERGROUND

If we could look under the ground, we would see rivers, streams, and even lakes. Water hides between rocks and in the soil just under the surface. But it can also be found at great depths. You might never see underground water, even though it's right there, under your feet. If it starts to decrease in any particular region, a lengthy drought can occur there.

Geysers

Deep underground, magma heats the water, which starts to evaporate. The steam rises up a vertical channel all the way to a crevasse or crater, from which it shoots upward, pushing out the water it meets on its way. The water and steam sometimes spurt as high as 200 feet. Some geysers erupt every few minutes, and others every couple of days.

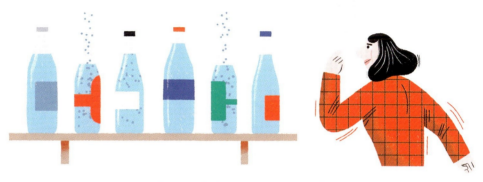

Sparkling or still

Some people like to drink tap water and others prefer bottled water, either sparkling or still. When you look at a row of bottles in the shop, think about what's inside them. The different kinds of water vary in composition, depending on the source they're from. For example, if they are from a place where there are calcareous rocks, they'll be richer in calcium, which helps our bones to grow. On each label, you can read how much magnesium, potassium, calcium, or other mineral salts the water contains.

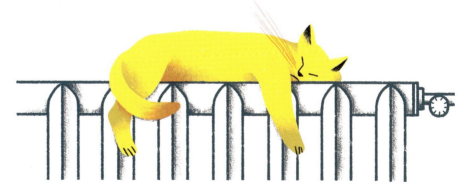

Geothermal energy

In winter, your radiator is hot because there's hot water flowing inside it. It can be heated by the city power station or by your own domestic gas boiler. It's also possible for the water to flow directly from under the ground. In some parts of the world, there are hot springs underground, from which hot water flows along pipes all the way to the houses, greenhouses, pools, and factories. It heats without the use of coal or gas. It is eco-friendly.

From outer space to underground

It's hard to study what's going on deep underground. So, how are we to monitor how much ground water we have? The best way is to travel into outer space and use a satellite. Specially designed equipment tracks the movement and volume of underground water. Naturally, these satellites cannot take photographs, but they can check changes in gravity, which is not exactly the same everywhere. Water has a lower density than rock, so its force of attraction is weaker. By observing differences in the strength of gravity and comparing results recorded at different times, scientists can estimate changes in the volume of underground water.

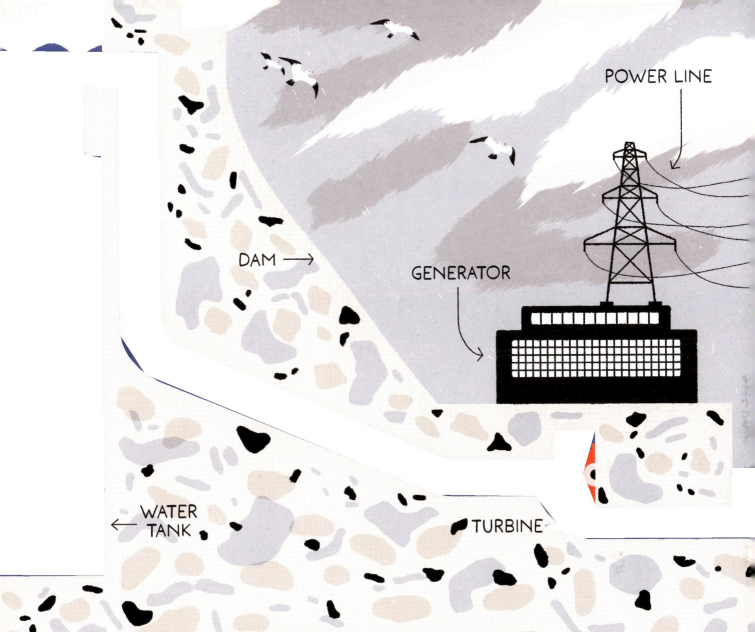

POWER LINE

DAM →

GENERATOR

WATER TANK ←

→ TURBINE

ELECTRICITY FROM WATER

Though there are fewer in use today, for centuries water mills have been powered by . . . water. But can water be used to light a classroom or charge a phone? Yes. All we have to do is to exploit its energy to produce electricity.

Hydropower stations are usually built on rivers. Dams accumulate the water, which then falls, activating turbines. Once built, this kind of power station is cheap, clean, and easy to service. As long as the river keeps flowing, it can be used to produce electricity.

Unfortunately, there can be downsides to dams as well. Creating dams by deliberate flooding means sometimes people—and animals—are left without homes. Dams also block the migration paths of animals. Salmon live in the seas and oceans, but each year they swim a long way up rivers to breed. They seek cool waters where the females can lay their eggs.

In some parts of the world, salmon migration has been obstructed by the construction of hydropower stations on rivers. The dam at Włocławek in Poland entirely blocked the passage of salmon, which fifty years ago could still be found in the Vistula River. To enable fish to swim past a dam, so-called fish ladders are constructed. These ladders have low, wide steps down which water flows in a cascade, carrying fish with it. Unfortunately, they do not always work as well as they should.

One of these fish ladders in the USA attracted so many salmon eager to swim through it that a traffic jam formed at the entrance. The fish soon became prey for sea lions that swam upstream to catch an easy meal. So, the dam workers started scaring the sea lions away, which upset defenders of the animals.

The world's biggest dam is on the Yangtze River in China. The Three Gorges Dam is more than 607 feet high, more than 0.6 of a mile wide, and almost 1.2 miles long. The electricity is produced by thirty-four generators. China is a huge country with an enormous population, so they need a lot of electricity. Most of it is produced using coal, which pollutes the air. The Three Gorges Dam produces green energy, but its construction has greatly altered the landscape. Such a large area was flooded that more than a million people had to be evacuated. Some ancient monuments and sites of interest to archaeologists were destroyed, and nature in the surrounding area also changed greatly. No one is entirely sure whether such large power stations bring more pros or more cons.

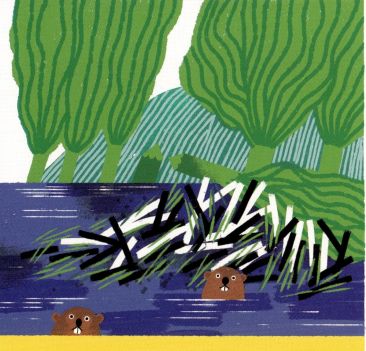

Long before we started to build dams out of concrete, beavers were making them out of wood. They cut down trees with their strong teeth and then use the branches to make elaborate barriers. Small lakes are formed, where the beavers can dive and build their homes.

The ebb and flow of the ocean can also be harnessed to light our houses, at tidal power stations. The water flows through the power station twice a day, activating turbines that generate electricity. The oldest power station of this kind was built almost sixty years ago in France, at the mouth of the Rance River near the Breton port of Saint-Malo. There are also tidal power stations in Ireland, Canada, and South Korea. By exploiting the natural movement of water, they do not pollute the environment.

THE ORIGIN OF WATER

Hydrogen appeared 370,000 years after the big bang, but oxygen only began to appear a billion years later, when a vast number of stars came to the end of their lives. They exploded, spitting into outer space the atoms of various elements, including oxygen. These atoms gathered to form interstellar clouds. Our solar system was created out of one of these clouds—a concentration of gas and dust. It was full of hydrogen, which now combined with oxygen to form water. The sun, planets, asteroids, and comets were gradually shaped out of all these particles and splinters of rock. So, it's possible that water appeared on Earth at the very birth of our planet. But the young Earth was a hot ball of liquid magma and had no atmosphere, so this water would have instantly evaporated and returned to outer space.

The water that fills the oceans today probably gathered on the Earth's surface only after it had cooled down and the atmosphere had developed. But where did this water come from? Scientists are still looking for an answer to that question. Thanks to research into ocean waters, they have discovered that some of it was supplied by comets and asteroids containing ice, which often collided with the earth a billion years ago. Another theory says that water came into being inside the planet, at an extremely high temperature and under immense pressure, as the result of a reaction between hydrogen and silicon dioxide (the latter is familiar to you as sand). While the volcanoes were taking shape it was forced to the surface in the form of water vapor. It is the main component of volcanic gases today as well.

For millions of years, no water has escaped from the earth, nor has its volume increased very much. So, we could say that we are drinking and bathing in the same water as the dinosaurs.

The big bang
The big bang is a theory about how the universe was formed.
But if you think there was a massive explosion that looked and
sounded like fireworks or a bomb going off, you are mistaken.
Instead, it involved the extremely rapid expansion of
all the matter of the universe, which had been
unimaginably compressed to begin with.

IS THERE WATER ON MARS?

In July 2020, the Perseverance rover was sent to Mars on board a rocket. It had six wheels, weighed slightly more than one ton, was 10 feet long long, and could move at a speed of up to 95 miles per hour. Its task was to examine the Martian rocks through twenty-three cameras, taking photographs and making videos that it sent back to base in America. Its radar studied the terrain, looking 33 feet below the surface, while other sensors used lasers and X-rays to scan the rocks in order to research their composition and properties. A special device can transform carbon dioxide into oxygen, which means it may no longer be necessary to provide supplies of oxygen from Earth for people to be able to breathe there. Perseverance also collected rock samples, which were intended to be stored in sealed tubes for a potential future mission to bring back to Earth. A self-assembling helicopter weighing just under 5 pounds also traveled to Mars on the rover, and its task was to study the weather on the Red Planet.

On the planet Mercury, water probably exists in the form of ice wherever sunlight never reaches, meaning at both poles, hidden in deep craters. As for Venus, many scientists believe that at one time there was water on that planet. Some think there may have been large oceans. However, current evidence suggest that any water would actually be in the atmosphere as vapor, with no liquid water present. Recently, some American and German scientists discovered that there is water on the surface of the moon. For the time being, they don't know what it is like and whether it could be used. But they're hoping the time will come when the astronauts who fly to the moon won't have to take water with them.

Do you think astronauts can simply pour themselves a cup of water? On Earth, water flows downward, because of the force of gravity. But in outer space, far away from any large celestial bodies, we have no sense of gravity, so there is no "up" or "down." As a result, the water won't stay in a glass, so the astronauts have to drink it out of small plastic bags, through little tubes. And if they squeeze it out of the bag, it forms the shape of a sphere that rises in the air.

Perhaps you're wondering what all this has to do with water. Perseverance was the fourth rover to set foot on Mars. Each one has persistently looked for signs of life. Maybe that's why its name is "Perseverance." Every space vehicle, probe, and crewless mission that reaches Mars is actually in search of water. They all gather masses of data about the rocks, the atmosphere, and the weather, and they send the information and pictures to scientists' computers on Earth. Here, specialists analyze them in the hope of discovering if there has ever been life on Mars, and if it would be possible now. So far, they know for sure that there is water frozen in glaciers at both poles of the planet. They suspect that there might be a lake just under 1 mile below the surface. And what if something were swimming in it? Perhaps one day this incredible research will prepare the ground for human beings to live on the Red Planet—and it won't be just science fiction.

CURIOUS FACTS

The world's three longest rivers are:
the Nile (4,130 miles), the Amazon (at least 4,000 miles),
and the Yangtze (3,915 miles).

The world's highest waterfall is the Angel Falls
in Venezuela. A stream of water pours non-stop from a
height of almost 3,212 feet. That's like three Eiffel Towers
stacked on top of each other!

The world's deepest lake is Lake Baikal in Siberia, Russia.
It's almost 5,315 feet deep.

A chain of volcanoes, volcanic islands, and oceanic
trenches stretches for more than 24,855 miles along
the coasts of the continents surrounding the Pacific Ocean.
Known as the Pacific Ring of Fire, this is where
earthquakes most often occur.

In 2007, the UK suffered from severe flooding,
caused by excessive rainfall. Millions of households
were without power and water, and the medieval
market town of Tewkesbury, Gloucestershire,
was turned into an island!

The most famous city built on water is Venice. It stands
on just over one hundred islands, with around 150 canals
in between them. The city's old palaces and mansions are
built on stilts and can only be reached by boat.

The world's longest canal system is over 1,000 miles in length and joins five rivers. At 2,500 years in age, it is very old! This is the Grand Canal in China.

The water in our bodies distributes nutrients (blood), rinses out waste (urine), and regulates our temperature (sweat). An adult human being should drink about 4 to 6 pints of water daily.

In 2004, some tsunami waves reached up to 50 feet in height. Approximately 230,000 people lost their lives. An earthquake had occurred beneath the Indian Ocean near the island of Sumatra.

In the course of a century, a water particle spends about ninety-eight years in the ocean, twenty months in the form of ice, two weeks in rivers and lakes, and less than a week moving in the air with the wind.

The fruits and vegetables that contain the most water are: cucumbers (almost 100% water), radishes (about 95% water), watermelons (92% water), grapefruit (91% water), and strawberries (90% water).

In various religions, water is a symbol of purification. Before praying, Muslims wash their faces, hands, and feet. Jews go to a special place known as a mikvah, where they have a ritual bath, but they also immerse new cooking utensils in water before starting to prepare food with them. During the baptism ritual, Christians drip consecrated water onto the baby's head.

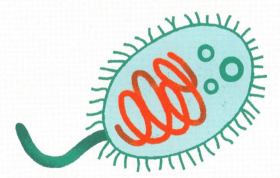

In the geysers on Russia's Kamchatka peninsula, the water temperature can exceed the boiling point of water (212°F), and yet there's life there in the form of some single-cell bacteria.

BOXER BOOKS Ltd. and the distinctive Boxer Books logo are trademarks of Union Square & Co., LLC.
Union Square & Co., LLC, is a subsidiary of Sterling Publishing Co., Inc.

Originally published as *Woda* by Muchomor, Warsaw, 2021
Polish text © 2021 Anna Skowrońska
Illustrations © 2021 Agata Dudek and Małgorzata Nowak (Acapulco Studio)
English translation © 2025 Antonia Lloyd-Jones
English translation rights arranged through KaBooks rights agency – Karolina Jaszecka

This edition first published in North America in 2025 by Boxer Books Limited.

ISBN 978-1-4547-1273-2

For information about custom editions, special sales, and premium purchases,
please contact specialsales@unionsquareandco.com.

Printed in China

Lot #:
10 9 8 7 6 5 4 3 2 1

04/25

unionsquareandco.com